WINTER RANGE

WINTER RANGE

PETER CHRISTENSEN

THISTLEDOWN PRESS

Canadian Cataloguing in Publication Data

Christensen, Peter, 1951 –
Winter range
Poems.

ISBN 1-894345-23-1
I. Title.
PS8555.H678W54 2001   C811'.54   C2001-910251-8
PR9199.3.C498W54 2001

Cover and book design by J. Forrie
Typeset by Thistledown Press Ltd.
Printed and bound in Canada

Thistledown Press Ltd.
633 Main Street
Saskatoon, Saskatchewan
S7H 0J8

  Canadian   Patrimoine
Heritage   canadien

Thistledown Press gratefully acknowledges the financial assistance of the Canada
Council for the Arts, the Saskatchewan Arts Board, and the Government of
Canada through the Book Publishing Industry Development Program for its
publishing program.

ACKNOWLEDGEMENTS

As I was writing these poems the thoughts and words of many writers came to mind. I acknowledge and express my gratitude to them and for the use of some specific phrases. Thank you fellow writers.

"Fencing Corollary" alludes to "How Do You Grow a Poet" from *Seed Catalogue* by R. Kroetsch. In "Orchards" I used the title words from Alistair MacLeod's book *As Birds Bring Forth the Sun* and in "When You Live in an Orchard"; "every robin that falls from grace" is a line from a Leonard Cohen song.

"GIS BS" was lifted directly from a British Columbia Ministry of Forests circular.

"Beware of Rattlesnakes" appeared in *90 Poets of the Nineties An Anthology of American and Canadian Poetry* (The Seminole Press, Sandford, Florida 1998 edited by John Garmon).

"Dangerous Work" was published in *Paperwork,* edited by Tom Wayman, (Harbour Publishing).

"Courage" was published in a similar version in *Borealis Magazine.*

"Brautigan's Books", "I Came Upon a Bear", "Courage", "Whitetail Lake", "Pilgrims", "My Father Who Art In Heaven", "These Two Friends", "Near the Little Big Horn River" and "Ox's Clothesline" were published as part of a chapbook titled *I Came Upon a Bear* (Writer's on the Plains, New Mexico Jr. College Foundation, 1996.)

"The Process" was published in *Stalking Place: Poems Beyond Borders,* (Hawk Press, New Mexico).

"Management" is taken from the libretto by Peter Christensen for the opera *Canyon Shadows,* music and production by Robert Rosen.

"Envy" and "Cutting the Surface" were published in *Sierra Sacrament* (copyright 1990 by SouthWest American Literature, New Mexico Jr. College).

"Slack Alice's" was published in *The Reader*, (Headbones Gallery, Vernon, BC).

I would especially like to thank Jennifer Gustar and Nancy Holmes at Okanagan University College for encouragement and time, the George Ryga Centre and Ken Smedley for a place to live and work and the Canada Council and OUC for providing a Writer-in-Residency where much of this manuscript was written. Thank you to Jim Harris at Hawk Press for publishing my work in chapbooks. Special thanks to John Lent who edited *Winter Range* and to all the wonderful people at Thistledown Press that have continued to publish my work, I am grateful for your support.

This book is dedicated to my partners,
past and present.

CONTENTS

PILGRIMS

Pilgrims   13
My Father Who Art in Heaven   15
Fencing Corollary   17
Courage   18
These Two Friends   20
Envy   22
Gravel Graveyards   23
Near the Little Big Horn River   26
Beware of Rattlesnakes   28
Terry   29
The Ranchman's   32
Benediction   34
Butterfly Effect   35
Happy Eggs   38
Whitetail Lake on a Sultry July Evening   42
Dangerous Work   43
Cutting Trail   44
Warden Lowen of the National Parks
   Service Gives a Speech of
   Encouragement to the Workers   46
Management   48
Break Down   49
Summer Sun   50

WINTER RANGE

We Who Hunted   52
   1. *In This Little Valley*
   2. *Keep Out*
   3. *They Say*
   4. *We Who Hunted*
The Early Adopters   56
Cutting the Surface   57
Tears   58

GIS BS   59
Truth Is What Walks Through the Door   60
My Dog Trixie   61
I Came Upon a Bear   63
Coots   64
Ox's Clothesline   66

THE MORAL ANIMAL

What Is Given   70
The Mathematician   71
Belated Frontier   72
Running   73
Culture Shock   75
Orchards   76
The Fever of Love   78
Gifts   79
Smart Like a Wolf   80
The Process   81
Touch   82
A Slow Day at Slack Alice's   83
Camera   85
Ache   86
This Is Not A Love Poem   87
Between Us   88
When You Live In An Orchard   89
Annie   90
Brautigan's Books   92
Through These Mountains   94

CODA: KNOWING IS HUMAN NOT OF RIVERS

When the Fish Stopped Coming   98
Imagine   99
Four of Us   100
Know Is Human Not of Rivers   101
The River Speaks   103

The superior man sets his person at rest before he moves;
he composes his thoughts before he speaks;
he makes his relations firm before he asks for something.

By attending to these three matters, the superior person gains complete
security.
But if a person is brusque in his movements, others will not
cooperate.
If he is agitated in his words, he will awaken no echo in others.
If he asks for something without first having established relations, it will
not be given to him. If not one is with him, those who would harm draw
near.

— Confucius

If faith does not reason, then it is nothing.

— St. Augustine

PILGRIMS

PILGRIMS

we are north of sign country
the roads have abruptly ended
there are no off or on ramps
our tourist maps are blank
shorelines waterways and skyshapes
are the only way
to find the place

this land is known to some
the local guides can show you
where to fish
when to fish
how to fish
when to run for home
when to go ashore and huddle by a fire
till tangled crests lie still

we four are pilgrims with some skill
who know each other's compulsion to risk
has brought us here
so we motor alone out of our bay
eyes turned up smiling rain
cleaning the lines in our faces

following the known ways
of the Cree or other pilgrims
we jig fat pickerel to the hook
build fires of gnarled boreal wood
fry fillets in salt and butter while
camped on granite shelves

on blind gray days intuition
a rough reciprocal bearing and
a little luck find the way to camp

storms reefs channels points of land
each must be remembered or

we will be lost in
the crimson smudge sky
above the endless shore in
the terrible balance between
fear and knowing

MY FATHER WHO ART IN HEAVEN

the wisdom of my father was
buried when
we set his coffin down
in that quiet corner of the graveyard
below a row of spruce and
placed a stone upon it

standing by the black hole
with my arm around my mother's waist
I did not know who supported who
knowing I should be strong
but I was not strong
in the face of everlasting peace
I cried and
took no comfort from
all the people gathered
to see my father
put in the ground
took no comfort
from the Pastor's words

for a long time
I did not understand
why his death filled me with anger
but I came to understand
that death had cheated me
of the chance to know him
as a man might know another man
a chance to be his friend
instead of a young male
full of himself full of answers
when in truth he had none

whom could I turn to
for counsel or comfort?
there is solace
in visiting the graveyard
his place, (as my mother calls it)
is surrounded by stones
bearing the names of his friends

strange to think that the dead
might have been lonely
that the squabbling at the door
is stilled by the knowledge
that all are equal in the name of the Lord

forever and forever
amen

FENCING COROLLARY

so you want to write a poem

do you see this digging bar
do you see this fence post
there is a shovel in the barn
bring it to me
together we will write poems

together we will turn this pasture
into a whole book of poems each
verse fenced by barbed wire
tight and strong so that
there is no escape

COURAGE

an ancient cathedral fir
fire hardened bark thick and gnarled
stands in a rock slide
its roots grasping the earth

a small boy climbs the primal wood
the sticky smell of pitch and heat
is adrenaline for his desire to
be above his will
he hauls his small body up the tree
one branch after another

near the top
his thin omniscient arms
easily surround the giant tree
in hot silence
his heart pounds
the proof of his existence

he raises his innocent eyes
looks out over the forest
down on the commerce of the valley
sees the highway
the house of his father

the wind sways fear into him
he clutches the trunk
knows enough of
God clouds and blue
blue sky

with a tremble in his knowledgeable hands
he struggles down to a thick branch
a safe resting place where
the golden tree is steady and
he is again enclosed by evergreen

he touches the earth
feels small and brave

THESE TWO FRIENDS
(for Glen and Jim)

these two friends I know
are on the radio
speaking poems of fish and friendship
their gentle voices swimming
the dark shoals of Jan Lake

it is as if
I am with them
standing by the fire Jim has built
against the cold offshore wind

its warmth crackles around our ankles
reaches up toward our outstretched hands
and pulls us down leaning back
we open our coats to
the slow heat of confession

I admit
I am unruly and isolated
too quick to argue
that contradictions and compromise
lead to imperfect people acting
upon a perfect world

I too have guarded the bitter flames
of envy and refusal

against the winds of forgiveness
history wove traps
my heart could not escape
I am ashamed to have wept
the thick and bloody tears of anger

o soft tongued friends
these confessions are of the fire
I beg you to stop my mouth
with gentle rags bind my thoughts
before they become maudlin

then soft as water speak your poems
your lapping admonitions
for only then will fish and friendship
calm this shrinking vessel
where I hoard your counsel

ENVY

envy the snake
his belly
so close to the earth

GRAVEL GRAVEYARDS

The Grand Forks cemetery
lies beside the highway
there are fresh graves
mounds of gravel still
above the horizon

each time I drive by
I am troubled that
this cemetery is made in gravel
not a single worm
could make a living
in such dry lifeless soil

for I take comfort
knowing decomposition
nourishes life
reason that as compost
we give back a little to
the earth from which
we have taken so much

but to be buried in gravel
seems nebulous as if
you'd be confined to
a pebbly conglomerate stasis

perhaps this is intended to
prevent one from getting comfortable
keep one fit for resurrection
or perhaps the parsimonious Russian
immigrants who settled here
could not bear to give up
productive land to graves

is this all there is at
the end of the trail
a hump of patted gravel
in front of a stone
if someone cares
a few dried flowers
twisting around
in an empty jar

for me, forget the box
I would like to rot in fertile soil
let the worms at me
the sooner a sunflower the better
or cast my shadow
to the wind
high in the mountains
to be at last
one with the fast boulder strewn streams
that I have wandered along
for so many years
what difference would it make
if this graveyard was made in loam
gravel ashes soil ocean or tundra

no one buried here
minds the traffic noise
only living creatures
can be comforted anyway
one's final resting place
is where the heart stops
and breath is let out

the only difference
it would make
is that when I drive
past the Grand Forks and
gaze across this gravel graveyard to
the grasslands of the Kettle River
then life and death would seem less disparate

NEAR THE LITTLE BIG HORN RIVER

east of the Little Big Horn
a field of winter crosses
lulls the rattlesnake to sleep
so we are at ease walking
among the bunch grass dunes

these scattered graves
tell a story of surprise and
futile retreat to this hilltop where
the cavalry circled their rearing mounts
to make a fort of human flesh and horses
before they fell to
scavenging warriors and ravens

at General Custer's Memorial Park
new rows of crosses
march down the hillside
laid out square as drill parades
they are for the young men
killed in foreign wars
a wilderness of bodies
transported to these bleak Montana hills
to make this graves' registry complete

all buried here are heroes
I am assured of this
by our wily information person
and I would never argue
the honour of the dead

but one thing is certain
not one of these underground will
trumpet the sage and wolf willow wind
blowing straight as a flag
down the Little Big Horn
under a shrouded winter sun

at the General Custer Souvenir and Curios
we browse but do not buy
in the car
out of the low icy wind
out of the ground storm
we follow the highway south

overhead a hawk cruises
tucks orange talons under his belly
raven follows the highway
in search of winter carrion
there is good winter camping along the river
shelter firewood water and graze

BEWARE OF RATTLESNAKES
(sign at the Little Big Horn Cemetery)

within the heated hollow of my automobile
I imagine a large rattlesnake
stealthily sliding
over cool cemetery soil
she tongues the furling wind for
scent of prairie dogs mice and men

unused to snakes and being a Christian
I am not easily convinced
to wander among lost lives or rattlers
I open my door cautiously
step into the graven winter wind

as I read the list of the dead
who gave their bodies to
the body politic
a sharp hawk cuts the grey hurricane sky
stones cross or grass
are equal to hungry eyes

as darkness comes crawling
the solemn sky
graveyard hawk and I
are reduced to work done
wars fought
time and soil

I slither into the warm car
snap the top off a Lucky
turn on the lights
drive away
my heart broken

TERRY
(In Memory of Terry Eddie, Saddlemaker)

the first time I met Terry
he was cowboy'n for Warner
ridin tourists round
the Circle Tour north of Banff
the next time I saw him
he was making saddles and tack
at the Bar J 5
said anything cut round
was either a Copenhagen lid
or a tobacco can lid size
made me a good scabbard
for my rifle

next time I saw Terry
he had his own shop
off 93/95
that morning he'd won half
of a $40,000 pick up truck
said
"I'm so lucky I'm scared to go to work
for fear of cutting myself"
made me a set of good hobbles
that do not sore my horse

next time I saw him
he was workin a suburban ranchero
on the Gold River Road
we talked about livin the life
who ran good horses or bad
who'd had a wreck

I'd brought him a bottle of homemade wine
and to my surprise he took offense

said beer was his style
said his wife would drink it
"just not something I grew up with"
made me a pair of good neoprene taps
that keep my feet warm and dry

I heard news about Terry
from a man who had worked with him
Ken said
Terry came on hard times
last fall he went to Alberta
to drive those lonely graders
on county roads
after a couple of shifts
he came home
went to his saddle shop
which was next to house
on the Gold River road and
hung himself from a beam
a customer found him
guessed he'd been there
a couple of days,
she never even missed him
Ken looked away and spit
said
it was the drinkin
and the woman was a ranch
he could not afford

what can I say for Terry?
a well made saddle will last a couple of lifetimes
or, those dam starlings will swarm and
peck at the wounds of a round knife when

love and money and distance
are held accountable

you stood in that grader
the sun baking your brain
as you took the roadbed down
one inch at a time
knowing damn well
Alberta roads held no answers

What the hell did you go and hang yourself for?

Terry will not be sewing new
backing and sheepskin on my good saddle
this winter like we talked about
someone else will get that work

Oh, I know one other thing to say for Terry
and that is
it is a great loss and nuisance
when a good saddle maker
who lives close to where you are workin
hangs himself

everybody said the poem should have ended
after the question
but I went on because
I thought Terry would have understood
there is a practical side to dying

THE RANCHMAN'S

he danced at the Ranchman's and called it a night
stumbled toward morning and then he got in fight
the dawn is a jail cell the crack is not free
if you wanna be cowboys better listen to me

he was a muscle bound hero he begged for his life
the cops came and got him he begged for his wife
to pay up his fines and take him back home
but he cursed her last night and now he's alone

o buckles and blue jeans and stampede corrals
you're just a high rider who is out with his pals
pack up your troubles and pay your debts down
take all your chances and get out of town

so make up a story while walking this town
dance that wild two step a country beat sound
he's a drunken bronc buster who lost all control
just sinew and muscles and gettin too old

the pimps they'll be lookin for gals on the street
whose fathers abused them the John's want fresh meat
o leather and buckles eighth avenue malls
you're takin a chance that the doors all have walls

so take up your saddle and bridle and spurs
leave all those junkies those boozers and curs
to fight with the law in the late night hotels
you know you're worth nothin your body it sells

at the Ranchman's the gals are all dressed up and tough
the boys are all heroes don't take any guff
it's an eight second fuse till the fights start again
the bouncers are bloody and all real good friends

o buckles and blue jeans and stampede corrals
you're just a high rider who is out with his pals
pack up your troubles and pay your debts down
take all your chances and get out of town

Yipee yae ki aa Yipee yae ki o Yipee yae ki aa ki o
Yipee yae ki aa Yipee yae ki o Yipee yae ki aa ki o

BENEDICTION

may your metaphors
be sharp as Mexican spurs
and your similes jangle
the belly of experience
may your words
ring round the pin
like the din
of a July horseshoe throwin' contest
may your eyes always
be as amazed as Renoir's

BUTTERFLY EFFECT

To my delight I found in my hand
a book of Wayman's poetry
it had been squashed between
the magnetic fridge poem book and
the multi ton locomotive steam pictorials
it was resting just above the spiritual sex manual
sandwiched by a rack of best sellers
and how-to books on how-to survive the end of the world
pressed tight by books about movies
massed amid huddles of eco psychology tomes
next to the hot tub how-to books computer manuals
log cabin notches gardening ball and puck sports fishing and
            hunting
reference books
just down the aisle
from the hundreds of lonely planet travel guides,
that make me feel oh so lonely,
across from the thousands of self help books
on the other side of the shelves stacked with history books
classics and yoga books calendars of motorcycles and cars hung
above the personal health
and not so personal health books which were flanked
            by books about cancer aids and cook books surrounded
            by thousands of books about objects and investments,
how to get them maintain them divorce them sell them
            or buy them

upon finding by accident this book of Wayman's
I cracked it open and read a poem
wherein Wayman buries his heart in the woods not far from
here
when I finished reading the poem
I blurted out
"There is not even a damn poetry section"

I said it so loud
that the clientele in the store heard
it just came out before I could stop myself
I know they heard because they raised their heads and
looked around in an uncomfortable way and
then a hush fell over the multitude of books
even the heavily reverbed nature muzak stopped
I think
and just for a moment
the vegetables fresh farm eggs and
lotto machine that pays the freight perked up
the owner of the bookstore looked over her glasses
from behind her till
the potpourri packets quit stinking
even the animalized card rack visibly shivered
then when all eyes had settled upon me and
all ears were turned toward me
I said
"No wonder Wayman buried his heart in the woods;
at least there was a little privacy, a little less information."
all of them solemnly nodded in agreement
even the books on PC World and Y2K stopped their callow calls
"Did Wayman leave directions to his heart's resting place
and why did he bury it in the first place?"
called out an individual onion from its wooden prison
I whirled amid the livestock and cat calendars
I could not believe what I had heard
and then in a chorus the books the clientele the lady at the till and
even the blathering nature muzak machine joined together
hit a big C major and sang in a Dylanesque New York drawl

"How could so many have said so much and still not have said it, man?"
(sing to the tune of How Many Roads Must a Man Walk Down)

I knew then I needed a cup of coffee
I slid Wayman's book of poetry back onto the shelf
between the steam locomotive pictorials
and the magnetic fridge poems
I hurried onto the erect street and quickly made my way to the cafe
where the young tongue troopers in their coded hair-do's and
long dark coats and ubiquitous pierced parts
were sanctimoniously milling

I sipped the froth from the top of my cappuccino
calmed down
suddenly I felt a burning guilt
for I had stolen a look at a poem
without paying for it
I dropped my head in shame
and then just off Baker street I rationalized
if I had taken that only book of poetry from the line up
then all literature would have been reduced to
information vegetables nature muzak potpourri how-to
and steam erotica
it would be as if
there was no poetry

HAPPY EGGS

I drove down to Keladen
to buy imperfect eggs
that must have come from
imperfect chickens
Free Range it said on the carton

you may ask why
I would go to so much trouble
to buy imperfect eggs

perhaps I needed
some grit in my life or
maybe as I struggle each day to
work off my after forty paunch
I could not bear to
shop in a store called Overwieghtea

and while those concerns were true
a more troubling question pecked at my heart
indeed an existential question
was scratching at my brain
you see I did not understand
why God had not made all eggs
perfect in the first place
if that was
where we were headed anyway?

could it be God made imperfect eggs
to give humankind something to do
after all with free range I mean free will
humans would need something to do
and having been given dominion
over the earth and over all the things that grow and crawl
well maybe

making perfect eggs would be
just the thing to keep us busy

I was fenced in by these fowl questions

I drove my Kelanden eggs home
and carefully set them on the table

as if reaching under a setting hen
I cautiously lifted the lid on the carton
and beheld a dozen different eggs
indeed there was a delirium of differences
some short some with small protrusions on their tips
round big ones next to small ones some tall and narrow
an unsorted bunch if ever there was

being a purveyor of metaphors
I was quick to recognize
that in this little paper carton world
multiculturalism although not official was
not a problem each egg was stable
I opened a second carton
and apoplectically viewed
a rather small blue oblong egg
nesting in the corner pocket among
eleven brown ones

in light of such anomaly
I felt sure that I would solve
this mystery of differences
but after a time
the problem remained ingrained
the answer had flown the coop

with one hope of de-scrambling this conundrum
I glumly walked to the Safeway store
and bought a carton of perfect eggs which
strangely cost less per dozen
than the imperfect ones
I took them home and
set the Safeway carton beside the others
I peeped in and
restless as a rooster
stared at the identical unfertilized twelvelets

slowly but surely a graceful comprehension nestled in:
the perfect Safeway eggs
were really the imperfect ones
for in selecting for perfect eggs
of perfect size and perfect shape
and perfect colour made by perfect chickens
these eggs, and the chickens that produced them
were made unhappy and vulnerable
for I understood that the slightest change of weather or food
wreaked havoc in the wired hen house and
all manner of antibodies are needed
to keep perfect chickens eating as they
perch precariously on rubbery legs there being
little difference between bone or gristle

and then there are esthetic questions   while
one perfect egg seems a thing of beauty
twelve identical perfect eggs are plain
and easy to take for granted
as if they have no story and come from nowhere
on the other hand

the free range eggs seem happy
even though their fate is sealed
unlike the perfect eggs they are content
and I speculate that the uncadged
unculled unregulated chickens

who roam the range and produce these eggs
are happy as well,
that is as far as I can discern
what is happiness to chickens

so could it be
that happiness depends on differences
that by being different we have
the greatest chance for freedom
for survival
could it be that God does not know
where we are headed
that we are free to range

I drove down to Kaladen
to buy some perfect eggs

WHITETAIL LAKE ON A SULTRY JULY EVENING

I had an evening on the lake
where lunkers drifted in the shallows
like living submarines
they swam in lingering curves
toward every cast I made
and gulped down my small blue dun
like after dinner wine

and as I set the hook
they danced like rainbows
across the still clear evening water
I played them one by one
these deep twenty four inch trout
and brought them to the boat
where my eager camera
stole their wet secrets

with a flick of my long nose pliers
I pulled each hook free from flesh or bone
and gently as wounded sparrows try
I stroked each fish slowly through the water
till reborn it swam into
the shallows and reeds to rest
above the marrow

DANGEROUS WORK

I turn to dangerous work
as a soldier turns to war
the body a divine target
testing luck over skill

falling the rotten wood or
hanging my life from ropes
playing the wild card
I think back to love

back to the pornography of the body
the exhibition of our desires
the graphic conclusion of animals

if any these will be my last thoughts

above us hangs a massive slab of snow
suspended in the tension of particles
fear ensnares me in a
world of physicality

humpbacked yellow machines
work the pit below
my nerve unfolds
I trust the ropes
there is danger
therefore
I am alive

CUTTING TRAIL

"You're okay until you step outside
after that you've got to be careful."

— Rob Toohey

in this green comfortable wilderness
I feel the forest around me
like a favourite coat
I know there are predators
hidden among the trees
grizzly wolf and cat
but I am not prey
so I bend to my work
clearing trail
turn my back on the bush

but then I hear a roar
and turn to watch
an avalanche of shearing wind
stampede down the mountain
ancient spruce whip like thin grass
the eye of the storm is on me
I flatten myself against a green balsam
and listen

understand now I am hunted
fear rips my itching belly and throat
pounds the walls of my chest
the yellow crack of a tree
breaks eighty feet of rotten wood
out of a giant spruce
it crashes lengthwise along the trail
where I stood a moment ago

then like grass behind a sickle
the storm has swept the forest calm
I humbly start my saw
divide the broken tree into chunks
roll them aside so pilgrims
can travel this trail in safety

WARDEN LOWEN OF THE NATIONAL PARKS SERVICE
GIVES A SPEECH OF ENCOURAGEMENT TO THE WORKERS

it was a day of packin fire hose
grubbin a line through rocks and
pine peckerpoles thicker than hair on a dog's back
by lunch we were dirty and hungry
I took a sandwich from my saddlebags
Warden Lowen says in passing
What the hell did you bring your saddlebags to a fire for?
everybody kind of laughed at me
guess I could have brought a paper bag for today

all afternoon we worked hard grubbin line
in the stones and roots and
then as evening settled down the fire
we packed hose into banana rolls
and threw the hardware in the crummies

tired and dirty
we were standin by the trucks havin a smoke
watchin a red sun dip below the peaks
when Warden Lowen drives up again
in his clean new government truck
in his clean uniform his tie on
he rolls down the window and
leans out of his air conditioned cab
a hard look on his face
his eyes settle on me
Warden Lowen says
You sure didn't make much of yourself, did ya
Christensen?
then he grins
studies the other faces

everyone got real quiet
kind of looked at me
like I should say something
but I did not raise my voice
I was going to tell him
I'd published five books of poetry
won some awards
given poetry readings all around Canada
and parts of the States
even published a story that won a prize
but instead
I just swallowed my pride
knowing there was no point to be made
I gave him a hard look
and walked away thinking about all that time
I wasted writing poetry

they say he'll retire in a couple years
maybe take an early buy out
a 75% pension
that would be good
cause I won't have to look for ways to avoid him
and maybe the new boss will think I'm holdin my own
for an older guy

MANAGEMENT

we are the managers
in the fast lane before dawn
circling the city

all is management
at work we shuffle paper
it is rustling grass
we rifle words and numbers
while resting at our desks
at noon we shop or rest

like a flock of birds from
red signals
we simultaneously drive
away from content

in the evening take our desire
home and watch television

BREAK DOWN

driving home one evening
I stopped
beside the asphalt
to wonder if we
were the only ones
who reckoned against dying

such finite beasts
we lap up the sun
swallow pieces of infinity
as if famine rages our bodies and
consumes our meager meal of time

the sun
abandoned me
day became night
in the dark mammalian warmth
of my car
I broke down and cried

SUMMER SUN

on this grey winter day
I do recall
high country summer sun
needle hot and burning
I shade my eyes
search the horizon
speak to my good horse
ask him to amble
across the ridge
so we can become
part of the alpine

WINTER RANGE

WE WHO HUNTED

1. *In This Little Valley*

in this little valley
we are in a way
all married to each other
no one is anonymous
crimes of passion
mistaken identities
infractions of the wildlife act
are remembered and tallied in
the grand community ledger

when change threatens as change always does
some are filled with envy
others hate

the new arrivals all believe
they have "discovered" this belated wilderness
where we have struggled
lived simply and fairly well
you can tell the renters from the owners
the first thing the buyers do
is nail up blood red NO TRESPASSING
signs to the trees and then
they build fences where no need exists

they have a need to defend territory
against others who seek the same solace
they have found and
like all colonizers once the fort is built
they become missionaries
act as if we who have lived here so long

are children
does this story sound familiar?
the oldest profession is colonization

I have become indifferent to these people
at times I resist or consider them fools
but I know there will
always be more
I will either learn to live with them or
go elsewhere

2. *Keep Out*

the little valley is filling up
with people who just got here
and want to keep others out

the more recent the arrivals
the more vocal they are
about keeping others out

they build barbed wire fences
where I used to walk or ride

sometimes the children of the valley
are sent away to urban schools
and when they return
they also put up signs
Strictly No Trespassing

and we who live here
wonder what they learned
about themselves that
they must now keep all others out

3. *They Say*

they say
that killing animals is wrong
unless sanctified by aboriginal claim
or the process of feedlots and abattoirs

they say
they have discovered The Valley
will save us from ourselves
they loudly lament the loss of the high country
while sinking basements and roads
into the winter range

at meetings
they
shake and furrow their brow
claim and profane their care
for the environment
seed hatred among us
quote Suzuki

they say
we should make doors and window frames
from what is left of the forests
get our meat at the fast food outlets
sit in our cars and eat

they will show us
how to live on the land

and like the industrialist's
their aggressive offspring

tear the fragile hills of the winter range
open to the weather with bikes and
All Terrain Vehicles

4. *We Who Hunted*

they say
we who hunted the bear elk and deer
must not hunt
because a percentage of householders
from town feel bad
about us killing animals

they say
the bear has an inherent right to live
that the bear is sacred
the bear is a renewable resource
the bear is an indicator species

they say
that the killing of bears is wrong
unless by the Conservation Officers of the Queen
in the name of
achieving the optimum sustainable population
or getting rid of garbage bears
or killing bears that are a nuisance
or have killed humans

and so that no one will profit
from this killing
like government surplus
the bear's body must go in the dump
but we who live on the land
know the bear is many things
and we know
we too are animals

THE EARLY ADOPTERS

the early adopters
circle the updrafts
sniff the rising air
eyes scanscopes
hunt prey
hunt advantage

but
preference is lost
as others swarm
bloating carrion
peck the bones

early adopters
ascend
on the
unflagging
stink
and

CUTTING THE SURFACE

if the rocks have no spirit
then you are the rocks
if the water has no life
then you are the water
if the wind has no heart
then you are the wind

TEARS

my tears are falling
tears are falling
tears are falling
the ground wet tears
look how the earth is
torn by my heaving breath
my tears are falling
tears are falling
tears are falling

just in case you ever wondered?

Geographic Information Systems
is a rapidly advancing computer based technology
where information is organized analyzed and presented
with reference to location

GIS is frequently described as a spatial process
because locations exist within space . . .

Conclusions:

GIS has proven to be of significant value
in economically integrating the different data sets
together
and is an extremely useful policy tool
in undertaking integrated resource planning
from the context of conflict identification and resolution
the key to sustainable development

GIS is a common denominator that
brings the different Ministries together
at the same time focusing the stakeholders
to make their own assumptions explicit
which then act to improve
the overall quality of the analysis

GIS provides the opportunity
for interactive testing of
integrated resource planning options
and can even be practical as a tool
for the presentation of dissemination of information
in a public forum context

TRUTH IS WHAT WALKS THROUGH THE DOOR

nowadays I have a hard time
finding perfect melancholy

a mood for writing poetry

the old edge between
hate and love
jealousy and generosity
rational and unreasonable
satisfaction and disobedience
anger and calm
relativity and relativism
you and me,
made me feel I could do it

now there is too much to consider
all is up for grabs
truth is market-driven
sage reminiscence just patriarchy
"cause the cat is out of the bag"
(who put the cat in the bag)
and stories are about power

nowadays truth is
what walks through the door
in the form of a facilitator
whose job is to evoke consensus
another kind of prison where
no one is allowed to disagree

MY DOG TRIXIE

"You're never alone when you're hunting with your dog"

how patiently the brown dog waits
circled in her winter bed
as she dreams and snuffles
the scent of sly birds
running under chokecherry thickets

how eagerly she waits
when in the field
she has found a bird
and holds a trembling point
till I am ready
for her
to release it

in restless winter sleep
she moans
for the Renoir days of fall
when we are finally free to wander
the Milk River coulees
amid the sage and rose
so few days we are allotted

how patiently she lingers
while I fire the cold stove
and then
languorously she rises
comes for her morning visit
I reach out
stroke her back

then predator to predator
we stare into each other's eyes
a shimmering pheasant breaks cover

and clatters into a straw sun
pumps the heart

she stands still   curves her paw
tracks the flight
waits for me to make the shot
before we plunge into
the brush and burrs
oblivious to thorns

I CAME UPON A BEAR

about a week ago near Spillimacheen
west of Jubilee Mountain
a local guide was riding
with his hunter
back to a deer they
killed the day before

as they neared where the dead deer lay
a 400 pound Grizzly charged out of the woodwork
and with one swat
took the hunter's horse down and killed it

the grizzly climbed on top of the hunter
and began to maul him
the guide was thrown from his horse
but still he managed to pull a rifle
out of the scabbard attached to the dead horse

he fired three times into the bear
while it was on top of the hunter
killed the bear
rolled the dead Grizzly off the American
bandaged him up
took him to a vehicle
then drove to the hospital at Golden fifty miles away

the hunter had 120 stitches in his legs

here we measure the severity of bear attacks
by the number of stitches sustained
that is if the person is still alive
if he is dead no one counts
I asked the guide if he was afraid
of shooting the man instead of the Grizzly
he replied
well I figured the bear was going to kill him anyway

COOTS

just north of Penticton
near a gray block bunker
where sewage spills into the lake
a barge of Coots
scud the whitecap winter winds

they seem content
to surf the eye of the storm
no one hunts these mud ducks
they do not migrate
are all one dark colour
no realists plagiarize their plumage
I would not eat one unless hunger drove me to it

Coots are numbered I suppose
but there never seems to be
too many or too few
and each evening
I turn north and watch
for this little flotilla of survivors
living on the edge of humankind's effluvium

it is good for Coots
if you do not
pour diesel down the drains
use acid to unhair your sinks
or wash with lifeless soap
I say this for the Coots sake alone
but who knows
one day you might be hungry enough...

now Coots as food aside
we could simply take comfort
in knowing
this little band of fighters
made it so far
that evolution for them
is water off a duck's back

OX'S CLOTHESLINE

You see, I received a thoroughbred mare as part of my marriage endowment and we were in a bind for a place to board her. Our place was not fenced yet so we approached our neighbour Ox about keeping Sassy at his farm on the nearby reserve. Ox had always been friendly, so we were pleased when he agreed to rent us a pasture.

One fine spring day I found myself driving down the Shuswap Creek road to Ox's to check on the mare. I parked near his house, stepped out of my truck and took in his situation. It did not take long to see that Ox was having a bad time getting his newly built clothesline to work. I observed that the line had come off the roller at the far end of his rigging. Normally this would not have caused Ox much consternation except with him having had a double hernia operation last fall and being sixty three years of age, he was contemplating whether or not he should climb up the tree again at the far end of the line and fix it. His gut was already sore from a full day's exertion.

As I viewed the situation, I could see that Ox had limbed his spar-tree from the ground up to where the line was attached leaving climbing stumps the full length of the trunk. At the lower end of the rigging was a platform about eight feet off the ground precariously perched along side the roof of his car port. Here the base end of the line was attached to a stout anchor pole.

The thing that gave this whole outfit potential was that this clothesline rig was long enough to hold the entire wardrobe of Ox's spouse, five children and the dozen or so foster kids which were nearly a constant part of his extended family. This clothesline crossed from one side of a small mountain valley to the other. The far end of the line was strung from a giant Douglas fir at about one hundred and twenty five feet off the ground.

I looked at Ox's malfunctioning high-line and then at Ox. "Are you planning to log the place?" I said.
Dead serious, Ox looked up and stared up to where the spar reached into the clouds. "This clothesline is for Marge."

Well, what could I do but volunteer to climb the spar tree and see if I could set the line back on the pulley. I wandered over to the far side of the little valley and began to climb. I climbed and climbed till I was high over the little valley. When I looked below, Ox was a smiling ant.

From this grand vista I began to understand the expanse of his thinking. This was the art of utility at its best. A clothesline high enough to avoid the neighbour's irrigation system, high enough to catch the breeze that flows down all valleys with small cool creeks in their bottom. High enough to get the laundry up into the weather systems. And long enough to do all the laundry at once. A masterpiece.

Even Christo with his pink plastic wrapped islands and draped canyons could not hold a torch to this fully loaded, cacophony of coloured socks, shorts, underwear, shirts, pants, dresses and towels. It was a celebration of cleanliness and tribute to the greatest clothes dryer of all.

The sun's yellow heat beat down charges of fresh ozone. The negative ions from the creek charged the laundry with such positive thinking that when worn, it would make you feel the pure natural pleasure of naked freedom in a wild place.

I understood that as Ox had stared down from this lofty platform the whole universe had drifted into place. He must have felt a sense of oneness with line, weather and utility. Just like Rosanne Cash had stated on the slip cover of Rodney Crowell's album. "At some indistinguishable point a choice was made. Art over celebrity. Language over formula. Poetry over politics. Out of this comes a passion illuminated by experience . . . real rhythm which shows us how to fall in love with our humanness."

High over the little valley, I settled myself onto a strong branch and with one arm desperately hugging the trunk of the spar I reached out and slipped the wire onto the pulley.

Ox, who had returned to the car port platform, shot the clothesline around the pulley pulling one lonely sock across the pasture up to within a few feet of my high perch. I took this podiatrist's flag to mean a kind of truce had been reached with the problem. Then cautious as a bear I slowly backed down the full one hundred and twenty foot length of the tree.

This gave Ox time to run across the little valley. He was waiting at the base of the tree when I descended. With a rather intense smile on his face he reached out and shook my hand.

THE MORAL ANIMAL

WHAT IS GIVEN

I feel heat

what is given

THE MATHEMATICIAN

you can prove pure math
but you can not test it
but it is beautiful
you have to choose your theory though
you have to choose your view of
how the universe was created
from there you can construct a world view
which can be measured and proven
and even function accordingly

if you decide that the distance from
0 to 1 is one kilometer
then you can go about measuring a flat world
based on that assumption
but what if the distance between 0 and 1
is based on a curvilinear arbitrary distance
then a whole other set of measurements flow from that

this choosing bothered me for a while
she said

BELATED FRONTIER

having come of age
in the belated frontier
I struggle to tend a bundle of ways
some would deconstruct

no show means no deal
a rescue party is not needed
be there or be unforgiven
hard rules for hard times
stay away from the bullies

I've made mistakes
took people at face value
believed their bullshit
I heard them talk
I interviewed burned-out men
in their bungalows
their health given to booze and cigarettes
taste the fruit
this is your future
if you buy in
make your choice

some things don't change
keep these animals
beyond the barrier

RUNNING
(for Cheryl)

running concrete canyons
running skin tight lycra
running to undo lunch
build energy
count calories
150
heart
beats
per minute

think about running
pass 4th the river
fresh water
run the body
to give up sorrow
to endomorphine
run the river's path
run past hate exhaustion
a good figure for fashion
look at me
120 – 130 – 140 endomorphine
get the pace
hold the struggle

does it matter
why not tell them
too much to lose
155 – 130 – 120
light change
walk the last block
concrete
bronze
glass

stop the whirl
hot shower god it is good to run
I am clean my skin good to touch
the dress shoes lipstick smile
all is good
look down into the canyons
100 – 90 – 85.
Good Afternoon
Yes

CULTURE SHOCK

Mallorca

black long-horned bull
auburn blood
gold sand
orbiting sun a welding torch
beer sangria tequila
lacey fans like roosters tails
cover the faces of rustling
catholic women

picadors
banderilleros
El Corodobes dances
barbed red cape bragging
hooked silver sword
butters deep
into the glistening black shoulder
sticks the cowed heart

a team of jangling donkeys
hauls the murdered flesh
around the ring
trumpets glare
as out the doors they prance
El Corodobes parades the ground
transcends a storm of roses
accepts two ears and a tail
all can see the kill was as good as in a lifetime

outside the gates in rubber boots
the butchers wait
at our hotel
beefsteak the special

ORCHARDS

these defiled and fecund orchards
in their summerland perfection
rows of ragged trees
hewn and pruned till
the complexity of their shape
is a function of their ability
to supply demand

there is little wild here
meager sanctuary
small birds return each spring
and bring forth the sun
nesting in the few old homesteads
where a spruce or a juniper
has been allowed to grow

this is agribusiness
pears are sprayed seven times before
they are assembled for the table
some apples mature individually
in sun filtering bags before
they are plucked for
particular eaters

I am lost in these orchards
search for metaphors
amid the fruit machinery
I imagine my life like these trees
first wild and free
then grafted to the stock
each summer
new leaders reach for wet heat
for the caress of wind rain and sun
for a season of shade

and sure as winter
the farmer cuts new growth away
the roots grow deeper
hope is a trick to
facilitate production

a fruitless trunk is salvaged
the chainsaw sharp and quick
roots plundered
thrown up to wither
in a desert of discontent
then burned

better to be born a vagrant bird
than an orchard tree

THE FEVER OF LOVE

the fever of love
has drawn me to
your hills and valleys

ardent lobelia blossoms
exhale a rosy musk

I caress the skin of the earth
inhale the animal smell
crave your cool carnality

urge your lust
so my fever of love
can be brought down
to normal

GIFTS

here I am
with a box of dark chocolates
to fuel your desire
here I am
with a red Valentine
inscribed Will You Be Mine
here I am
a bouquet of roses in hand
flowers that satisfy

I bring these gifts
because the sun
has been aroused

I yearn
for the destruction
of my winter feelings
for heat
I bare my desire
expose my belly
turn my cheek

SMART LIKE A WOLF

When, in the course of its evolution, a species of animal develops a weapon which may destroy a fellow-member at one blow then, in order to survive, it must develop, along with the weapon, a social inhibition to prevent a usage which could endanger the existence of the species.

(Konrad Lorenz, *King Solomon's Ring*)

the wolf has enlightened me
he turns his belly up to the aggressor
not to surrender
but because he knows
the aggressor cannot attack

I am determined to love
to have my cup half full
to be amazed
we are less violent than we are
to believe we are moral animals
by will and not selection
I am determined to believe this
even though I lack evidence

THE PROCESS

we were beautiful once
lived as artists
suffered for a while
were famous

I know we lost our ideals
the war to get money
breaks
the easy body down
lines rake my forehead
crowsfeet corner your eyes

I grow accustomed
to headaches
unseen ailments

I no longer have my pantheism
to keep me cool
under the hot sun
of nationalist religions

I have learned to vindicate
the affairs of the heart
with alcohol
various prescriptions

I am a crucible
in which to give up dreams
dogma is strong medicine
I can change nothing

TOUCH

all these damn poets are
is feeling
they can't even look at the weather
without crying

they just follow
emotions around
as if that was all
that matters

like dogs at the heel
they do not analyze
but
their passion
can be effective
point to the heart

sometimes
their empathy for possession
is so strong
that a few of them
will even retrieve
once the emotion is down

A SLOW DAY AT SLACK ALICE'S

all the women who perform
at Slack's
engorge their breasts with silicon
their nipples always erect

one after another
they loll about the stage
taunting the men below them
who stare up into their pussies
suck their drinks from straws
whistle for attention
and imagine
she would be
available to cook
just for him
upon demand

I am too cynical
should just enjoy a little bump and grind
for the pleasure of pleasure
these women will tease
the men will please them
with money
if they are able

but not many here seem happy
not the men staring up at the stage
not the bartender or the waitress
not the sullen single men at tables
who stare into their drinks
not the stripper
who has attached a chain
from one nipple to the other
and down to her vagina

there is only one group
of men and women huddled round a table
whose faces are at ease
none of them engaged by the show
they lean forward towards each other
are telling stories and laughing

CAMERA

have you ever noticed
no matter if
She
runs walks drives or dives
that the American camera
is always focused on Her breasts
unless She is running away
then it looks at harass(sic)
on the other hand
if He
shoots or boots
somebody
the camera looks Him in the eyes
or stares at His weapons
ejaculating lead into the competition

ACHE

in Summerland
the women
are lovely to meet as
they drown slim glasses of amber beer
talk philosophy and feminism and
ache with loneliness

but where are the men
are they all bitter fruit
or doddery
have they been finished off
in one conflagration
dust to dust

consigned to the workheap
to worship labour and productivity
spending their lives like
cold blooded horses?

in Summerland women
come and go
wondering what became of David

THIS IS NOT A LOVE POEM

there are lonely women
who visit us and privately offer me their bodies
but ownership is final
unless we split the blanket
so I must love all women in you

these women
need love
would settle for a few athletic nights
and I might oblige them
because they want what you have
because there is a chance
that I will want their body
as much as yours
because they want to come
with a friend

maybe I should oblige their restlessness
just to feel new earth new cities beneath me
but I turn down the offers
or tell them to discuss it with you
which none of them have

though I fantasize
about some temporary fucking
it is with you I have my contract
during storms and calm

this poem is not a love poem
it is about desire and need
about compassion and contract
success and failure
it is about saying yes or no

BETWEEN US

I stare at the grey limestone wall
in view from this cabin
deep in the hills
it is clear and hard

it is the fever of your tongue
I long for

WHEN YOU LIVE IN AN ORCHARD

when you live in an orchard
you know there are seasons
when birds go hungry
when farmers rake
the barren trees
from the earth
like worms
into the mouths
of greedy robins

I do not believe
that God keeps track
of every robin that falls from grace

you say your body
is the territory of grief
are sick of loveless men
parading their seed

I pity them
that they are not much
in your eyes

love
what does that mean
a tangled animal in barb wire
I cannot unsnarl

ANNIE

while riding the chair lift with Annie
she asked me
what are you gonna do
I said
live off my wife
she is supporting me at a lifestyle
to which I would like to become accustomed
Annie became silent

to ski you must
become one with the fall line
this is the zen
but Annie could not forget the pain
she brought with her to the mountain
and she carved my comment
close to her heart

at the end of the day
I brought the car around
she threw her skis into the trunk
threw her poles at the back of my seat
got in to the back of the car
and slammed the door

I asked
if she had a problem
she huffed like an angry bear
and said
it's called teamwork
I don't know what you would do without Yvonne

this caused me to think
she believed I was useless and dependent
and I admit my anger got the better of me

Annie I suspect you are commenting
on something that is none of your goddamn business

well that kind of broke the ice
later we said we were sorry

but you see how just one little story
can turn the heart
harden the arteries
tighten the lips
just one phrase
can twist the knife

The wet heavy overnight snow had crusted on the horses backs. They are shivering. I grain them for warmth and then chase them out to the meadows below the cabin. A strong down wind rushes in from the glaciers. I'm sure they're relieved I am not insisting on another traveling day in bad weather. Our gear and selves were thoroughly soaked in yesterday's ride, so today we wait and dry out.

Inside the warming cabin, I hang my dripping yellow slicker behind the cook stove. I stuff enough split wood into the firebox to keep me warm for a couple of hours and put another armful of wood into the oven to dry. I pour hot tea, stir in a teaspoon of honey and settle at the kitchen table next to the window to read Brautigan's *Tokyo-Montana Express.*

As I read I can't help looking for clues to the reasons for his death. I find nothing in particular; in fact he has me laughing out loud at times, but still I can not help thinking this was the work of a man without hope. Brautigan was a great observer of how he himself thought and of his surroundings, but there did not seem to be any values attached to his observations. Yin or Yang. It didn't matter. To die or live was the same?

It made me speculate that maybe the North American mind does not deal well with Taoist philosophy, with contradiction or fate. Brautigan developed his sensibility to accept the earth and its inhabitants the way they are, a universe unfolding as it should. I feel an intense sense of chaos. Without any traditional values or rituals, close extended families or feudal allegiances to give him stability and cause, perhaps he lost hope. Maybe Brautigan decided he could no longer care when others did not. He accepted chaos and the anarchy that is art, completely. He took refuge in form, in allegory and in parable but I guess those were banal and then he took his life.

Without reasons to care, life has no meaning. Without meaning, there is no reason to create. Some say we create to give life meaning, be it gods, war, machines or ritual. But if even the desire to create is gone, then surely a person feels helpless.

My back shivers, the fire has burned low. The room is cool. I raise my head. It feels tangled, like a horse that gets into bog with heavy packs on. He cannot struggle out of the bog because of the weight on his back and he cannot remove the weight himself.

From out of the storm I hear one of the horses whinny. I go to the porch and look out over the meadow which now has a white limitless feeling. The whirling snow, shadows of dark clouds and changing winds give a ghostly appearance to the horses. One of them must have lost scent and sight of the others in the storm and called out.

Suddenly the storm opens. I hear the thudding of hoofs nearby. Bells clang. They are coming in to be fed. I pull on a sweater and rubber boots, throw my long slicker over my shoulders and walk to the oat shed. As I walk I recall what an old horseman told me. He said, "Horses will always come through camp before they pull out. If you get up, get out there and catch them, grain them and close them into the corral for a few hours, you'll have horses when you're ready to leave."

THROUGH THESE MOUNTAINS

through these mountains and valleys
is the way back to you
back to the struggle
to make what we have work
it is clear
that you are worried
frightened
that our love
is ending
as you leave
you say
I love you
but it is a question
as much as a statement
so sharp
and accurate
that a slice of doubt
is silently known
as soon as the words are

before you leave
you instruct Anna
to take a picture
of us
in front of the crumbling Mexican archway
leading to the rambling old house
amid the orchards
above the lake
where I am writing
where I face my demons and demagogues
desire reason and uncertainty

the picture is evidence
that we were here together
this too is our house

you must go now
to work
for the corporate giants
the ones who have taken
so much of our lives
given us money
as you leave I see fear in your eyes
uncertainty in your smile
I do not say
don't worry
for I am caught up
in these spring orchards
caught up
in all this pruning back of life

the way back to you
is through the high mountains
there are passes rock falls
torrents and dark valleys
but I know the road eventually
becomes singular
reason virtue and passion
join together
lead to the doorway
into our small house
high in the mountains

Coda: Knowing Is Human Not of Rivers

WHEN THE FISH STOPPED COMING

after the damming
the fish stopped coming
so the men of the town
changed the name from
the Salmon River to the Salmo

they argued that there are
too many rivers named Salmon
why not drop the n
and lose the irony
in the name of a river
once full of fish
now empty
and distinguish our river
from the others

IMAGINE

steelhead swimming
the Columbia River
the Kootenay River
the Salmon River
to spawn
in gravel estuaries

their saline flesh
falling from their bones
freshets
to nourish cottonwoods and bears

Hidden Creek, Wildhorse, Lost Creek,
Whitewater, Porcupine, Sheep Creek,
South Salmon, Stagleap, Rainy Creek . . .

imagine these vessels
cooling the molten earth
making rain
imagine these rivers full of fish

FOUR OF US

four of us climb
along Hidden Creek
white noise so constant
that only Water Ouzel song
can pierce the spring roar

a pictogram on granite
two ochre figures
arms spread wide
"big fish, big fish"
says Alice
on Hidden Creek

at the falls we humans
ponder risky Water Ouzels
building their nest
on a rib of stone
a foot above high water

we are silenced
all the while the river speaks

KNOWING IS HUMAN NOT OF RIVERS

the river does not care
what is put on it
does not see or hear
or feel tired or needed
does not go to work
need money or care
if the job was bid
too low or too high

the river does not feel
cold or pain or
broken in spirit
make mortgage payments
enjoy fine wines,
excess, desire, passion,
cool thoughts,
anger

a river is dammed
its energy seized
channeled into wires
it does not feel sorrow

the river does not care
if we live or die of cancer
or stroke or lung disease
are fit or mentally ill

the river does not care
if we sewer it,
smelter slag its gravel beds,
dump salt, garbage, pulp effluent, 24D or rain . . .
it flows or doesn't flow
clear dirty polluted or stinking
it's all the same to the river

the river is not subtle or riproaring
or easy or difficult to run
the fishing is neither good nor bad
the river has no memory
no conscience no history
fought no wars lost no loved ones
the river knows nothing
knowing is human, not of rivers

THE RIVER SPEAKS

Dippers build a nest of moss
sing a tune to pierce
the raging stream

Harlequins romance the river's edge
take flight
as we drift old water

a deer sips the swollen stream
we observe through river eyes
that she is thirsty

the boatman is busy
in the river with his oars
we are free to watch

underneath the Salmon River
a Dipper grasps the stones
feeds along the bottom

nymph and stonefly
birds and fish are family now
that we have heard the river speak

science commissions art
both are astounded
renaissance in a dark age

the river in harness
pulp mill, hydro, highway
a city full of people

the hills are stripped of wood
torn open
we are warm in our houses

the river is dammed and dammed
and dammed
we watch television

wild fire lines
leave trees along the creeks
erosion is prevented

turtles sunning on a log
dive for weedy cover
harmlessly I float

a school of nervous fish
fingerlings and fry
harmlessly I watch

the river with all its problems
the discontent
with all their solutions